Living
in the
Fire Nest

Poems by
Linda Nemec Foster

Many of the poems in this book were previously published in the following magazines and journals. Grateful acknowledgment is made to all the editors of these literary reviews:

The Georgia Review, Nimrod, Midwest Poetry Review, Indiana Review, The Chowder Review, Passages North, Tendril, University of Windsor Review, The Bellingham Review, Laurel Review, Invisible City, Wayne Literary Review, Menomonie Review, Exquisite Corpse, Labyris, Another Chicago Magazine, Sierra Madre Review, Croton Review, Luna Tack, Quadra-Project, South Florida Poetry Review, The Sow's Ear Poetry Review, Milkweed Chronicle, The Worchester Review, Manhattan Poetry Review, The MacGuffin, The Pennsylvania Review, The Garfield Lake Review, Korone, Visions International, Renegade, ONTHEBUS, Blue Buildings, Farmer's Market, Eleven, Michigan Broadsides, Permafrost, The Bridge, Brix, The Burning World, Parting Gifts, Mid-American Review, Artful Dodge, Sky, and *Green River Review.*

The author would also like to thank the editors of the following anthologies where some of these poems appeared:

Contemporary Michigan Poetry (Wayne State University Press), *Concert at Chopin's House* (New Rivers Press), *Passages North Anthology* (Milkweed Editions), *Women of the 14th Moon* (The Crossing Press), *Dan River Anthology,* and *I Am Becoming the Women I've Wanted* (Papier-Mache Press).

"Fragments of Athena" appeared in the collective art/poetry exhibit *The Fear of Women* (Michigan).
"The Woman Taken in Adultery" was selected to appear in the national visual art/poetry exhibit *Passion* (New York).
"Men as Fathers" was selected to appear in the national visual art/poetry exhibit *Hope* (New York).
"Chinese Acrobats" was performed in the stage production *Still Life with Conversation* and was published in an anthology of the same name by Ridgeway Press. Many thanks to Rebecca Emlinger Roberts for her support and unique vision.

Some of the poems in this book have been previously published in three limited edition chapbooks: *A History of the Body* (Coffee House Press), *A Modern Fairy Tale: The Baba Yaga Poems* (Ridgeway Press), and *Trying to Balance the Heart* (Sun Dog Press).

Special thanks to the Michigan Council for the Arts for its support. Two poetry grants awarded by the Council were instrumental in the completion of this manuscript.

Published by The Ridgeway Press, P.O. Box 120, Roseville, MI 48066

Publisher: M. L. Liebler

For Tony

Contents

And the Love, Just Beginning

The Thin Air of Dusk

A Modern Fairy Tale: The Baba Yaga Poems

Under the Rim of the World

Prose Poems: A History of the Body

And the Love, Just Beginning

Old Lover

Look how she sits there:
head bent towards you
lips delicate on a cigarette,
and you don't notice
the curve of her leg,
the small hand trying
to balance your heart.

You begin to forget her hair,
her eyes, how she smells
when her body is close and tense.

Now she merely waits for you
to notice her green dress.
All the gray air
leaves her mouth;
once you wanted
to die there.

The Wife of the Fireman

She's the one who rarely sleeps,
thin lines of her hand foretell absence,
it smells heavy, black:
air that is not air
wrapping itself around him in a house
where another woman waits to be held
and carried to a safe place.

With his wife lies that part of him
always dreaming of wet grass
and a broad tree with a sparrow
nesting its young. She never enters
this dream but sometimes she appears
so close to its edge that he fears
her breathing will wake him.

She's the one who rarely sleeps,
who creates half-dreams that fulfill
prophecies of a baptism by fire. Shadows
turn to flames when she hears the sirens:
her hair singes and grows shorter
her body erased by the heat he lives for–
her bed, swallowed and emptied.

Landscape in Fog

This street you've lived on for years
becomes a blind alley, your house
succumbs to the terror of being
another's. Even your wife seems
to belong to the man next door,
her fingers caught in the damp
air around his bed. Those sounds
of common comfort also escape,
and you cannot recognize the familiar:
your footfalls, your voice, the pattern
of your shallow breathing.

When the fog lifts, it pushes you
out into the clear world;
you can see the hand
before your face, unbroken
lines of the palm directing
the same course. You can hear
that song your wife invents
as she threads the empty
eye of the needle.

The Long Ride Home

The long ride home
after strong coffee,
black pepper ground
for our salads, and
the edible syllables
of women's talk:
that we are wives
with husbands who search
moist earth for our imprint,
some clue they can trace
in their sleep; that we
are mothers of children
who, having left our bodies,
continue to leave us.

After all our excuses,
the long ride home—
just that and nothing
more; not even darkness
or the bright moon.
It melts in this summer
heat. Already, a tiny
sliver is missing;
its drops will find
shelter in the hollow
of our necks, our necks
that husbands
will taste in the morning.

What the Magician Tells His Wife

Nothing that can possibly
interest you. Dear, dearest.
My sleight-of-hand, a series
of foregone conclusions I
rattle off in my sleep.
Red silk scarves growing
into white rabbits growing
into stiff peonies from my
thin hands. I am lucky
I do not sweat much.

But you, balanced in a blue
sequined leotard, black fish-net
stockings gathering your legs.
They really watch you.
None of the magic matters
when I chain your ankles
and wrists. Place you
lovingly into the dark trunk.
Casually thrust heavy swords
through your neck, your heart,
your groin. And make you
disappear.

What magic can top the audience's
own, when, for that longest
of split-seconds, they feel you
consumed by the very air. Breathe
you in, allow their bodies
to possess you before I
bring you back–
unchained, whole, visible.

The black curtain trembles
as you materialize.

The Sirens

The sea belongs to them: it rises
and falls with their every glance,
submerging whole mountains, caverns
under its cold blue weight.
While above, in the air, the sea's
bitter sweat tries to drown the birds
that fly so close to your boat.

You watch these tired gray wings
and hear the sound of hopelessness,
the last breath;
but who really believes it?
The sun still promotes mirage,
subtleties of light and mind,
and the wind still speaks in tongues.

Are you listening? Good
because soon they will come to you,
braiding hair into nets, their breasts
the perfect bait to suck:
and you will
and you will love it
and you will believe anything.

Their song is that good
you know the melody
long before the air does—
the rhythm so complete
it can hide darkness
or the ruins of men,
the small bloody traces.

Dreaming in a Foreign Language

I dream the Tower of Pisa and St. Peter's Basilica
are in the same town. Small, cluttered, everything
on top of one another. The buildings gasp for air,
the trees drown the houses and streets. We're together
and I'm amazed at your closeness, your fingers
in my hair. I hold your body as if I could hold
it forever, a postcard I could send home and keep.

Some noise disturbs us: in front of the art museum,
a parade squeezes through the narrow streets. No bands
or baton twirlers, just large Romans with classical noses
clambering up the thin road, their horses as big as houses.
Every one of them is determined to find their women
recently re-kidnapped by the Sabines. They look mad.
They look like their cocks have goose bumps. You glance
at the city's skyline and Pisa's Tower drops an inch.

Inside the art museum there are high school nuns
who moonlight as gallery guides. They smile and silently
take you up the marble stairs two at a time. Their black
stockings escape from ankles, lead up to invisible
regions that probably don't exist. Embarrassed, you
look out a fifth-story window and see the Tower
leaning toward you–a medieval Godzilla crushing trees.

Your beard gets caught in the heavy, wild branches. You
swim in leaves and want to eat my accent, the European
vowels that hesitate before passing my lips. You keep
your fingers matted in my hair, hoping to claim me
at the border, high in the mountains where the trees
cannot follow and you feel safe. Ice and rock
in your mouth. Safe. But I'm like Daphne, stuck
to the ground, and the roots won't let me go. I can
reach higher than any tower and I won't let you go.

This cramped town will preserve itself like a fossil
in the veins of the leaves, the lines in our palms,
the strange language we speak that neither of us knows.

Now the Romans are coming back with their horses
loaded with women. It's going to be hot
and dripping. Everything on top of one another.
Your words leave your mouth so slow,
a tree could grow faster. I shake my hair free,
place leaves, perfect holy symbols, on my breasts.
The first rituals before going home.

The Devil at Chartres Cathedral

The thirteenth century needed you
to stand by the portals.
Your long ears the motif
as you remain balanced in stone,
an aesthetic forming grace.
You hold women by the legs
carry them off like Sabines,
their hair trailing behind
covering your tracks,
those delicate hoofs.

Your work never diminishes.
That soul around your neck dangles,
forever close to your church door.
It cannot resist you,
the smile between your legs
so charming it makes nuns blush.
Your tail brushing the back
of their heads, soft strokes
the only thing touched.

This power you possess, two faces,
their tension serves you—
the sharp grin in your head,
the lush smile growing out of the loins
where your cock should be.
That one is the killer, friendly,
not even a tooth visible,
not even capable of piercing
those women you drag behind.

Old Sarsaila, old dark master,
the poison is there, pleasure
that settles in the dark brain,
your genital/face knows,
keeps on imagining more:
sins beyond flesh and memory,
your smile so calm
damnation cannot deform it.

The Woman Taken in Adultery

In my opinion, there's something
inherently boring about fidelity.
Whether to one man, one God,

or one country, a body stagnates
under the pressure of the solitary
existence. No life after this one

can be worth such virtue.
Instead, I'll opt for the man
who cuts my grass or my brother-

in-law from Phoenix or who-
ever happens to win the men's
championship at Wimbledon this year.

Even the paper boy is fair game
as I count every coin in his
back pocket; I'm prepared to seduce

all or nothing. And if eternity
greets me with closed arms and
the judgement that if you lust

once in your heart you've sinned twice,
I'll get down on my knees, unleash
my hair and beg to wipe his feet.

The Red Shoes

They tell me I dance good:
they, of course, are the men.
In high school, on the weekends,
beer blasts in college and those
secluded boat houses veiled
in dust. Wherever I danced
they followed: Cleveland to Detroit
to the other side of the Great Lakes
and back east through Pennsylvania,
upstate New York, lower Manhattan.
I am responsible for teaching
the entire population of Vermont
how to forget those precious
mountains and dance dirty.
I did this on five separate
occasions and never got paid.
Down along the eastern seaboard
and two-bit Jersey, inconsequential
Delaware. My reputation preceded me
as I stalked D.C. and its heavy-
footed stomp, the moist Carolinas, hot
Georgia, oppressive air of Florida
that I danced in all the way
to Key West and all the way back.
Waltzing through Tuscaloosa, Biloxi,
and wet New Orleans. My toes
sinking in the silt for relief, only
to be yanked out by the next
partner offering to lick my soles
clean before the music started
the foxtrot, rumba, or slow
two-step. Missouri, Chicago, Iowa,
the repetitive plains and mountains
and ocean. The contagious states.

The boring list of places that over-
run the map; nothing holds more
space in the whole universe.
Except for my tiny feet. Now
you want your turn. Will you
settle for an ending instead?
An ending that reads: don't
take me too seriously when I
move with your body so good,
fucking couldn't be better.

Fragments of Athena

"the great goddess hacked
into tourist souvenirs"
Eve Merriam

If I'm so smart,
what am I doing here
in Nashville at the fake
Parthenon greeting the plodding
tourists from Wisconsin
and competing with Dolly
Parton's chest? I tell
you, I'm dead. Don't
believe all the lies
in the brochure: that I'm
born again in the largest
indoor sculpture in the Western
world. Complete with Nike
balanced in my gigantic
right palm. What these 20th
century Americans won't
do for culture. Not that
they want ancient wisdom
or even modern wisdom.
Only answers, facts, the bare
minimum. Why do women
open their mouths while
applying mascara? Can red hair
cause memory loss? In mechanical
terms, is the dentist's drill
a direct descendant of the wind-
mill? I'm not making any of this up.
These are the questions that explode
from their minds when they see
me, bigger than life, bigger
than anything in their lives.

I'd rather be tiny, miniscule
like a black figure against
a terra-cotta background
on an amphora from Naxos.
But I'm stuck here
with the couple from Milwaukee
and their kid who wishes he had
X-ray vision so he could see
the secrets between my legs.
And I'm not the only
woman caught off-guard.
Imagine the picture of three
headless goddesses silkscreened
in neon on a T-shirt that
a urologist from Kentucky
happens to be wearing. I know
about these modern times. Laser-
surgery performed on big bladders.
Akin to the entrails studied
by the Delphic Oracle. Really,
your world is not that different
from mine. Men still blow
us away, bit by bit. First
our brains, then voices, then
glowing souls–all overwhelmed,
silenced, buried. Until
we're sitting on our hands
like middle-aged debutantes
or standing in frozen replica.
You ask me about fear:
woman, go look in the mirror.

Housework

The fact that your mother loves it,
automatically makes you hate it:
her obsession for ironing underwear
and hankies and bed sheets. She cared
whether or not you had a crisp crease
in your white panties. No matter
that it was invisible to everyone else.
Scrubbing the attic floor once a week
and the dishes five times a day
left time for nothing else, which suited
her just fine. And the fact that you
spent infinite hours composing term papers
and got a master's degree from some
uppity New England college that no one
in Ohio has heard of means nothing
to her. Who cares if you can read well
or write better? The window sills in your
house are still cluttered with dying
plants, dust, chipped porcelain.
No husband. She reminds you with every
refusal to come and check for herself.

Absurdity of the Sweet Life

In the living room my television blares:
"This evening's movie, complete and uncut,
is Fellini's classic, *La Dolce Vita*."
I stand in the kitchen fixing dinner,
the usual: boiled potatoes, green beans,
meat loaf. Getting the beans washed
takes precedence over Jesus flying
through the skies of Rome, arms lifted.
Now Marcello and Anouk screw in a whore's
flooded apartment and I'm still
in the kitchen. I don't even see Anita's
big entrance. Is her blond hair up?
Is she wearing dark glasses? I overhear
a question from the Italian press:
"Is it true you take a bath every morning
in ice-cold water without any clothes on?"
Her tremendous breasts (they're all thinking)
could heat up anything.

                         The television's
still blaring when my husband comes home
from work. He forgets about dinner,
about his hunger, about his anxious day,
as he sits mesmerized by Anita. Her flowing
blond hair, black, strapless gown, those
breasts. Now she aimlessly wanders the night
streets of Rome with Marcello at her heels and
a white kitten on her head. She's in love
(with the kitty, not poor Marcello) and
places it on her fair scalp, its tiny tail
brushing her forehead. My husband is certain
there's going to be a nude shot as the dinner

starts to burn and Anita finds a big fountain
to plunge into, a big fountain her big tits
can push out of, but nothing happens.
The black, wet, strapless gown still clings;
the body remains hidden; the dinner is ruined;
my husband grumbles. Nothing happens.
If Jesus could finish that helicopter ride
and touch ground just once more, I wouldn't
ask him to perform the miraculous, but only
the ordinary. To land in front of the stove,
finish stirring the beans and potatoes, and
not forget to turn-off the meat loaf so I
could watch *La Dolce Vita* from beginning to end,
not miss a second of some other life's sweetness.

Drought in Suburbia

Another day of no rain,
strong heat, stagnant blue
in the sky. The man
in the air-conditioned
house is depressed.
Not for the farmer
in Kansas, seeing his
stunted corn wither
like October leaves
at his feet. But for
his own lush green
grass reduced to flat
brown straw. Every evening
he uses six sprinklers
to water the lawn. His
wife says it's hopeless.
The next morning dawns
cloudless with more straw
surrounding his house.
Only the white sidewalk
looks content and radiant.

Birthday Poem

Our fathers' slow climb
up the stairs.
How the city was hot,
August, and hard to sleep:
men can't dream easy
in such heat;
only search a little
for their wives lying still,
lying closed, then open.

And this hot night is for you
as well as for me.
The white cotton sheets stained–
our father's sweat, our mother's skin.
We were born out of them
almost on the same day,
probably conceived that same night.

II.

1949 already owned our parents.
The post-war upward move:
suburbs and green shrubs,
plastic flamingos on a neat lawn.
Their thin legs balancing the marriage
that lived in the house beyond–
completely brick, mortgaged.

Days of afternoon factory-shifts:
each wife understanding
nothing but this first pregnancy,
her husband's body laid bare.
Each morning almost sinful
when she felt too sick
to get up and clean the house.

The nights forgave again and again:
a bird of blue grass, perched
in a white shadowbox, would find the moonlight
and fly through dust.

III.

Twenty-two years for each of our lives.
This celebration has no candles
for lovers who almost share birthdays,
share dark nights in a rented room
where the only light comes from the stars–
stars that shape a goat, a virgin.
We shape the twins but not as brother/sister
and refuse to believe the predictions:
we will become dangerously similar; Gemini
in each of us will destroy the other.

But we cannot escape the one fate
that began with our parents'
slow movement in the same darkness,
which bore us, pushed us out,
into the air of a late May night.

Not our close births but our close lives
will prove the harder miracle.
Eye to open eye witnessing
how small we sometimes look,
how terribly lost and common.
And the love, just beginning.

Contrapuntal: The Dance

You make it look easy

        This pattern of ritual

as you push your weight so close–

        forcing me to follow

the language of bodies

        is endless. How we touch

has no preference for details:

        that bone, that muscle determines

only the one last act

        a sense of direction, our longing.

Love Poem

for Tony

She discovers she is in love
almost by accident tripping
over his body in bed finding
strange underwear between the sheets.
She must now readjust her habits:
no nightgowns or 11 o'clock news,
take off the glasses, don't
forget the Pills. This list
grows long, thick, cumbersome
until her mind becomes heavy
and her neat, square jaw softens
into an indistinguishable but loved
face. Perhaps she should dye
her hair blond or red
or blue—some tangible evidence
she didn't completely sink into him.
But it's useless. When he comes
to her again, tonight, she will open
the door, shed her dress, take her
once solid heart and place it
in the deep, quiet well of his hands.

The Secret House

"The history of architecture is
the history of the struggle for light . . ."
Le Corbusier

For years, he plans their dream house.
Studies building and design from borrowed
books at night. Learns the difference between
fuses and circuits, wood sash and casement,
lap joints and dovetails. He buys an old
farm house on the north end of town
and tells her: "Potential, think potential."
As if she could ignore the rotting wood,
clogged plumbing, the electrical wiring not
up to code. So they think potential and
move into a green-shingled place that chokes
on eighty years of oiled paper on the windows.
Each year, he tackles a new project: stripping
the wood to its barest grain, ripping up
the basement's foundation, tearing the walls
down past the paint and plaster to reveal the lath.

For years, they live in a half-made house,
a crumbled bedroom that neither of them
wants to sleep in. At night, they dream
different dreams. His are always about
being able to fly–as casually as a moth–
above the rooftops and oak trees and his wife's
white laundry hung out to dry. Hers are about
being on the ground–actually under the ground–
in her mother's root cellar where no light
reaches her. The only sensation is that of sound:
hearing the ball dome lids pop on the quart jars
of tomatoes, pears, applesauce, and currant jam.
A voice calls her name, but she never answers.
Morning comes and they rise from their dreams
of the sky and the ground to face another day
with walls torn down, old yellow wallpaper fading
like someone else's memory, the dust lingering on.

And what does the woman do when there is no house
to call home? She has babies to pass the time,
makes clothes for them and their dolls. Intricate
smocked dresses with pink roses and brown bears.
Elaborate suits with coats and vests and pockets.
She keeps a loom in their bedroom and on those
nights when she cannot sleep she weaves shawls
of deep mauve and ochre and gold. All the colors
that don't surround her. Finally, after four children,
they slowly begin to reclaim the house and
mold it into their own. A new basement is dug,
an addition is put on the back, the bathroom
changes locations and becomes new. And,
the premier room in the house is finished: her room—
the kitchen with lilac blue formica on the counters
and solid oak cabinets. A new stove, sink, dishwasher,
a refrigerator that gives her ice and cold water.
But still she feels uneasy. What to do with all
that needs to be done, and once it is done,
what to do with that inevitable calm in her life.

In the middle of a June night, she awakens,
walks around the house, finds herself staring
at the kitchen floor. There, reflected on the white
linoleum is the moon, beaming with no effort
from the new skylight. She is amazed by its closeness,
by its total lack of desire. How it so easily
finds its way through the elaborate hole
in the roof and settles at her feet. Like one
of her sleeping children, like an unexpected house
guest. A woman in supplication who secretly
wishes her prayer will never be answered.

Untitled

In her dreams, it is always cancer.
A beautiful, wild flower waiting.
The nurse announces the diagnosis
without fanfare, like an ambivalent
Gabriel proclaiming a terrific beginning
or a terrible end in the same
dull monotone. The surgeon
quietly enters from the corner
of her left eye and removes
her right breast with such cool
abandon–as if a breeze moved
through her body, as if a river
flooded its banks and eroded the earth
that had slept beside it for years.
There is no pain, there is no blood.
Only wind and water rushing
headlong through her.

Before the anesthesia wears away,
her husband's face hovers above her.
He is holding the breast that doesn't
belong to her anymore, cradling it
in his palm as if it were a lost bird
that has fallen out of its nest,
that has forgotten how to sing.
He tries to teach it the music
it once knew. What escapes
his lips is nothing but the echo
of bare trees in winter, calling
her name through the thin ice.

Throwing Old Things Away

Once a year you open all the closets,
seek out boxes, finger locks on trunks
that have no memory until you empty them,
until those years of high school are so real
you don't feel married and nearly thirty.

You hate it: not the going back
but the coming forward into the present.
Another raise in rent, a best friend's divorce,
tendency towards migraines and those days
where you have to convince yourself again
and again–yes–throw out the yellow dress
or the light green cologne that made some boy
love you or even the letter you never
sent him that could have changed everything.

You want to believe that boy is still there
just outside the door, waiting on the stairs,
returning each year to hold you.
But he never stays long enough;
you are always too obvious,
awkward in your attempt to seduce.
And he finally leaves, embarrassed, quiet.
You do not even hear him on the stairs.

The Thin Air of Dusk

Nightmare

I'm the one with the madness
stuck in my throat, the dry lips
of the last man shot at dawn.
I'm the one you least expect
when the dream hatches in the room
like larvae changing into furniture,
ordinary chairs. I'm the man
perched on the ceiling, smooth
and far away. I'm the woman
with the painted lips bending
my mouth over rosary beads:
a string of skewered coal
I place around your neck.
I'm the deformed child
growing from your shoulder,
your shadow, the yellow
breath you exhale. I'm the fire
trapping you inside, your feet
the dusty floorboards that won't
move. I'm the scream that refuses
to leave your mouth and
your mouth a gaping hole
that redefines the idea of black.
I'm the murmur of gray walls,
the windows talking to themselves,
the mirror that cracks easily.
I'm the estranged lover with a knife
cutting through your reflection
to reveal absolutely nothing.
I'm the fertile wound that keeps
bleeding, bleeding while the rest
of your life sits on its hands.

In the Belly

Jonah,
what you doin'
in there?
All white
from whale breath and
no one the wiser.

Trapped in a belly
so big it
might as well
be God's, you
strike a match
and see ribs
the size of Babylon's
hanging gardens.
Solid muscles move
all around your
little head wrapped
in seaweed,
packaged
for breakfast.

Are you scared,
Jonah?
Try to look out
of the big whale
eye for some
glimpse of land,
solid ground
filled with deep
roots and deeper
bones, unmistakable
clues that you are
not yet dreaming
of the one death you
will wear in your sleep.

Here there is no
night, no day,
no mermaids
with arms, lips.
Only you
with unblinking eye
and God
with a closed mouth.

The Last Week in Lent

Rumors strain themselves
over sidewalks, changing
the air with their gossip,
curving tongues around trees,
birds, the first green leaves.

And in the sky, these same words
touch the gray and embarrass it.
Quiet breath that comes slow,
that holds blue in its mouth
announcing the tomb empty,
the winding-sheet folded,
and the women standing as silent
as their jars of myrrh.

The hard earth never listens
but feels the movement of deep roots,
wants to believe, just this once.

Song of Red Candles

We're red holy wine,
not to be found
on high altars or
lights near martyrs.

Our desires are dark and pagan,
born when lions crushed
babies' heads;
the state sold tickets
and we cheered.

Got drunk that same night
and swore to live forever.
Our muscles pulled back,
white tongues easing out–
back/forth we burned,
burned.

Now we exist, waiting . . .
to feed on your coarse hair,
that secret ground
which is black and moist,
deep and old. We live
in the empty catacombs
of your latest dream
where you fear
being touched,
discovered,
dragged away.

Sister, don't
blow us out; the candles
in your bedroom shine
like blood let loose
from your dearest wound.
Take hold of the flame,
melt with us.

The First Death

Your death was my first glimpse
of a young face in a coffin
made-up to look quiet and alive.
I did not recognize the rose dress,
cameo ring, or small crucifix,
only the long hair on the white pillow.
You planned it that way,
never wanted to cut it:
"short hair is bad for my health."
True—you couldn't afford
any more bad habits but that hair
almost concealed other vices:
the heavy drinking and bad temper
that cold night last winter.

In December despite a foot of snow,
you wanted the corner bar, promised
not to hustle, not to play the game
even if they offered to buy.
But you drank too much again,
caused a scene, a big black man
hoisted you into the air, laughing:
"just one tiny wet kiss."
You got mad at the cigarette machine,
pounded on it until the metal knobs
left their imprint on your hands.
Stigmata, you smiled and showed me,
making sure to leave blood behind
so no one would forget you.

But all this can't matter,
you are dead, the long winter gone.
From a glass of booze or a high ledge
there is no real difference.
Both result in that last tremendous fall
the same wind hitting your lungs,
the glorious moment when your hair
begins to grow on its own.

Detroit

for Jan Zayti

A city like Detroit only exists in a prose poem. No stanza or line break could contain it. But paragraphs–big blocks of words–that's what Detroit is. Run-on sentences border its streets, parking lots: heavy miles of guard rails and fences. Cars live here: carburetors, catalytic convertors, automatic transmissions, power brakes, power steering, white side walls, fuel injection, radiators, front suspension, mufflers, bucket seats, leather, chrome, head room, leg room, ride like a million, can we build one for you, the highways of your mind, luxury ride, down 8-mile, 7-mile, 6-mile, 5-mile, down till they don't count no more, down to the Renaissance Center, and the mass transit that nobody gives a shit about, down to the very guts which is not blood or heart or even steel but riding fast smooth down the leg of Woodward Ave., windows open, radio blasting. Keeping alive.

Instinct

Red berries survive in winter.
A proof we deceive ourselves
in believing the season's ice
only destroys
the insignificant life.
Dull, invisible sparrow.
Anonymous deer frozen
in the field.
Incoherent drunk
lost in some alley.

And how we endlessly attempt
to be free of any danger
by attempting to be wise
in our houses—
sitting by fires,
windows closed,
our blood warm
and predictable.

The small birds have nothing
to do with our wisdom.
They merely fly
in the freezing air.
Do not know the laws
of improbability, the risk
of fragile wings.
They only understand
the survival of berries.
Their eyes obsessed
with dark fruit,
the deep color still
vibrant when their thin beaks
crush it easily.

Sanity

The man reclining on the edge
doesn't dare lose balance.

Breathing between the heavens and the earth,
he prays the stars seep into his eyes,
he prays the ground stays still just for him.

In the dead of autumn when his tired bones
move like empty branches, he will lie down
among naked trees. On his back, he views
the universe like some hushed blue parlor.

The fact that the tops of the trees
are upside down chandeliers–
their clear prisms broken by the sun,
defying gravity–
doesn't bother him at all.

Jesse James at the Osceola Inn:
Reed City, Michigan/1884

Pure legend. Fictitious as this boring land where lies
flourish. But who in this small town in northern
Michigan would know that by 1884 he had already been dead
two years? So the front-desk clerk with pale
green eyes and city-bought cowboy hat talks
up the only story that keeps him and this town alive:

how Jesse slept here. And you listen, wanting Jesse alive
again. Thin lips, blue eyes, the face of a girl that lied
about anything. The soft-spoken voice that talked
the love of Jesus in a Missouri Baptist church where "north"
might as well be "hell". The delicately pale,
almost womanly hands that should've thumped a Bible, not
    shot dead

the 19 year-old boy at that first bank robbery. Dead.
Like Jesse's little brother blown to bits by a live
grenade. Or his gang members caught and lynched with pale
rope. But not Jesse. He lived the full breath of the lie
pulp magazines relish. *REBEL GUERRILLA STILL AT WAR*
    WITH NORTH
read the headlines. And North meant Big Business, Big
    Money, Big Talk.

All useless against the man who invented the train robbery
    by talking
himself into it. Who robbed banks during business hours
    not in the dead
of night. Who waited for 9 years to marry a cousin
    from north
Missouri that happened to have his mother's name. Who was
    barely alive
as a husband and father, whose wife almost escaped his
    attention as she lay
next to him. The moonlight finding his body awake, pale—

fearing to dream the nightmare of Minnesota. How the pale
August sun made Northfield simmer like a mirage. Its women
    talked
of heat. Hardly noticed the disguise of land speculator,
    the lie
that got Jesse into the bank but not out of it. Later,
    the women counted the dead
in Main Street as if it was their civic duty to keep alive
the memory of dull husbands. The store clerks and bar
    owners of Northfield

who in twenty minutes destroyed the gang that held the North
and South spellbound for a decade. The image of Jesse, pale
and wounded, touching his face and asking it: "Are you
    still alive?"
He had six more years to keep answering *yes*, to keep talking
to himself that his life mattered. Even though the
    flamboyance was dead,
the gang was dead, and in a way, he was dead long before
    the lie

of Bob Ford's gun. And the front-desk clerk is so alive
    as he talks
about Jesse sleeping in this northern Michigan hotel that
    you cannot look into the pale
green eyes. This man in this dead town curving into himself
    with nothing but the beautiful lie.

Tabloid Headlines

for Gary Eberle

The woman with two heads
can't decide whether to have
an abortion or keep the baby.
If Elvis isn't in Kalamazoo
belching burgers at a road-side inn,
pieces of his brain are floating
amidst the cosmic dust of the Crab
Nebula. While a jungle guide
is eaten alive by 6-foot tall
killer ants, a woman from Idaho,
weeding the garden in her back yard,
is abducted and becomes
Big Foot's Love Slave.

Each of these random miracles
vies for the attention of the man
who shops for Tuesday's dinner.
Like a buzzing halo of gossip
that encircles his tired head,
the tabloid headlines glow
with the familiar made unfamiliar–
the sublime, commonplace;
ourselves, pulp.

Up and down the aisles, he fingers
eggplants and zucchini, eyes the petite
veal steaks and frozen orange roughy,
smells coffee grounds and crushed oregano.
He wonders about his life. His little
life that will never make the tabloids
unless he gets pregnant,
dines with Liberace's ghost,
or lands a UFO on the White House lawn.

Even the girl behind the cash register
is bored by him. Her eyelids glow
with luminescent colors–
jade shimmering into silver, then sapphire.
A fish-eye, he thinks. And he remembers
that mermaid caught in the North Atlantic
and eaten by a hungry fishing crew.
What part did they eat first? Fish-tail
or torso–the long hair, thin arms,
round breasts? If he was there
on that boat, one of those fishermen
hauling in the strange catch, would he
prepare the meal or cut loose the line?

The question follows him past the automatic
sliding doors, into the parking lot,
into his car where his own life sits
waiting for him in the approaching
dark of the back seat.

Postcard

A magician from Germany sends me a postcard.
In halting English, my language foreign
and untenable to one who's mastered the silent
sleight-of-hand, he writes about my poems.

They remind him of a tight-rope dancer
(not walker). A tight-rope dancer balancing
between two myths of understanding: the light
and the dark. Such praise from a stranger.

And so this postcard: a picture of a tiny woman
on top of a 19th century automatic clock. She holds
a balancing pole, peeks out of a tree whenever
the hour is struck, and attempts the tight-rope.

She looks like Snow White or Our Lady of Guadalupe
except for the men at her feet. A tiny quartet
playing a melody I cannot hear: lute, tambourine,
trumpet, snake rattle. All of them dolled-up

in crimson and gold-leaf waiting for her to perform
her stunt. Waiting for everything and nothing
like purveyors of eternity usually do.
But in the picture, she's frozen. It's 4 o'clock

and the men just want it to be over, this balancing
act, until the next hour announces itself.
Of course, nothing happens. Except for the wild tree
behind her, offering a splay of brown leaves.

The huge trunk embracing her like a gaping wound
as if it were a grotto at Lourdes or Fatima.
And she, some miraculous vision balancing between
who-knows-what. The magician says he knows.

But he won't tell me. Or maybe he can't.
Given the space limitations of a postcard,
and the risk of communicating mere words
to an absolute stranger. And I think of him,

on the other side of the world, making magenta
scarves disappear at whim and white birds flutter
from empty hats. Holding my poems in his pale,
foreign hands until they become the thin air of dusk.

Bon Voyage

You're going to Paris, the city of love,
without your husband and the night
before your harried departure
you have a dream so guilt-ridden
it makes your hands sweat.
Inside the dream, Paris looms
like a rude, unwanted dinner guest:
guzzling the Chardonnay; smearing
greasy lips on the linen napkin; spinning
the bone china dinner plate in a perfect
trajectory under the host's nose.
Nothing in Paris is famous anymore. The dream
tells you this whole trip was a mistake.

Not even bumping into an old boyfriend
on the Champs Elysees can cheer you.
He's dyed his hair red and become an artist:
"Look," he crows, "I've got the black
clothes to prove it." He's in Paris
to study with Rodin and create light
sculptures heavy with the abstraction
of thought. A hard act to pull off,
especially since Rodin is dead.
This doesn't seem to bother him but
you do, with your uncertain French accent
and sweaty hands. So you leave him
standing under the Arc de Triomphe looking
like your father before you were born.
Skinny, smiling, a stranger with the wrong face.

That's when you wake up next to your sleeping
husband and desire only the familiar:
the cool dirt of your garden, the common
weeds that have overtaken the front yard,
the smell of coffee on the breath of your
only daughter. Meanwhile the dream continues
to unravel with Paris waiting for your arrival
like an impatient blind date. The boy
you never dreamed of till now.

Michele in Japan

I.

You have been gone for five years
country girl on an island
living away from a friendship
we shared too quickly
for permanent words to form
now you send long letters
greetings from Kyoto
the many ghosts of war
lying in your bed, you dream
try to imagine the farm
the oak tree
the pregnant cow.

II.

For my wedding, you sent
the only gift, a porcelain face
a lover's mask from a No play
white skin/red lips/the eyes
black, slanted holes
your look exactly
as if it was your face
your mouth parting the lips.

III.

Night comes first to the East
the moon living in ancient temples
adds to the darkness
the stark eye of white
and you approach it
this night like the others
try to cover it with your hands
the sound of the other half
calling you calling
as real as your children.

Chinese Acrobats

A man in red silk pajamas sommersaults
backwards with bad news. Tanks in
Tiananmen Square and blood in Beijing
have altered the contour of his mouth.
Each foreign syllable, which has crossed
time zones, an ocean, and two continents
to get on stage, suddenly freezes like
the thin air of Tibet. The small woman
beside him tries to balance a huge jade
vase on her delicate, raised foot, but
it slips. Jade slivers of light everywhere.

This light does not illuminate
the fate of two girls on their knees
before the gate of Heavenly Peace,
bayonets fixed at their throats. Or
of the young soldier whose face
was torn away by the mob on Changan Ave.

The broken pieces of light only reflect
an absence of weight: what is left
when plum blossoms fade, green willows
break, the tiger becomes extinct–
the empty sound of an audience's applause
as their blind, mortal hands find each other.

Climbing Harney Peak
Black Hills, South Dakota

for Bob and Therese

The rain lasted all morning,
ending in a mist, its silence
more complete than the rocks.

We start the climb after
the clouds break, leaving a blue
that defines the very edge of things.

Half-way to the summit, we stop,
drink clear water with cupped hands,
our mouths touching the stream.

For the Lakota tribe,
this barren place of black trees
was the center of the world.

At the top, we finger its scars:
graffiti, broken glass. The abandoned
air and dark pines breathe through us.

Below, the world is invisible.
Our children, all those we have named,
impossible to know from this height.

As we descend, the mist returns
to claim us. How it knows our voices,
our very shapes. So little have we changed.

Poem for Four Children Dead in a Fire in Detroit

That one night you shone
brighter than the moon
and for miles we saw
your light in the sky
afraid to ask what or who

but the smoke could not mask
the blue veins stuck there
rotten house good for rats
mother good for nothing
life could be more cruel
than letting you smoulder
the chair half
out the window blazing
the dolls looking
with melted smiles
blue eyes almost ash
your tiny limbs black
wave through the broken glass
then suddenly, the final
animal teeth exposed

you are now smoke
rising above the house
slowly entering this dark sky
all around you the stars
live in their fire nests

The Dream Reinvented

In last night's dream, I became a gray sparrow
nesting in the oak tree outside my daughter's window.
I spoke in the quiet light of evening.
I knew the meaning of her name,
my ears attuned to her voice.
I saw my reflection in her eyes and learned
the song she taught herself in my absence.

In last night's dream, I wanted to speak
in the forgotten language of clouds.
I watched the sky for patterns, for advice,
and forgave when it offered only the wind.
The leaves said it was enough.

In last night's dream, I feared the waking world
of no wings, not even a remnant of feather
in my new hand. I moved in sleep, in the eye
of the dream, and felt my daughter's blue gaze.
The oak tree whispered: Go back now and sing.

On a Picture of Rilke

You look out from the flat page and think
deep blue or women, those joys never with you
are more soothing than delicate hands on lace
or the heavy smell of a gray suit.

After reading seven of your books,
I'm finally convinced this strange face is yours;
oblivious to the tight collar, you sit calm,
think of Russia, Venice, countless trunks.

You don't care about the mantle clock
behind you, the uncomfortable straight-backed chair
or that heavy Bible balanced on your lap,
awkward, cumbersome. You were never holy.

But you are afraid of this room where
I live and breathe and hold you casually
along with those poems that tried to shape air,
to embrace angels before they died.

On their graves it must be raining. You
know how it feels: wet air, perfect loneliness.

Zambia: Women Drying Fish

In the picture, there are two of them.
Strong, brown, their hands
casually sort the silver rows
of Kapenta fish as if no other
world existed beyond this table
of dried reeds, the southern shore
of Lake Tanganyika at their feet.

Each woman has a small child
slung at her side, kept in place
by green swatches of linen.
The child on the right, an infant,
has fallen asleep while nursing
at his mother's engorged breast.
The milk dribbles past his open mouth,
past the green linen,
anoints the fish drying in the sun,
becomes another part of the landscape.

And what's beyond that sapphire sky
if you could peel it away?
Even the great mind of God
could not imagine the impossible:
a brittle brown twig resembling a girl.
Her black hair has turned
burnt orange, her mouth begins
to fill itself with dust.
And her hollow eyes reflect nothing
but the lights from hundreds
of lanterns on fishing canoes
as they circle the silver Kapenta
lying just below the surface.

Lost

Mistaking New Hampshire for West Virginia,
how could we forget where we were?
Place ourselves outside of Charleston
when outside our car it was Manchester.
Mistaking one state for another–pure and simple.
On any journey away from all that's familiar–
beds, smells in closets, even a personal method
of accumulating dust–our minds cloud over
like rain that hasn't quite fallen. A thousand
shades of green become the same green. A singular
blue dominates the sky. And, after a while
(shorter than we could ever imagine), mountains
are transposed without a hint of difference.
The White Mountains are indeed the Appalachian.
Don't laugh. This may not be high drama
but it's serious business enough. Losing a sense
of place is never as frightening as splitting atoms,
but for us, lost ones, it might as well be.
We will never find the cemetery where an aunt
buried her seven children. Could be anywhere now.

A Modern Fairy Tale: The Baba Yaga Poems

The Unending Vigil

In villages near the Caucasus
men whip their women's legs
once a year, in the spring
to bring fertility
to allow sweet juices to flow
the constant vigil against barrenness.

And she watches from the cornfields
hair tangled, covered with husks
her mouth climbs the stalk
and stays there
devouring small pieces
veins of the leaves
green beginnings
of another life.

Baba Yaga

I.

Your hut stands in the darkest part of the woods
revolves in circles until night swallows it
in the villages and farms people lock their doors
light candles to keep away the dark
all the evils that come begging on two legs.

Old woman, you come so quick
souls of the dead don't have time to cool
you roll your skirts high, higher until
your teeth are visible, the ones between your legs
sharp edges that gnaw and tear.

Your victims are caught in a web of trees
and you, the spider, stroke them with legs
legs so hard that the flesh barely covers.

II.

Day and night are your servants
white and black horses
they come to your door
smelling of earth and rain.

You braid time into their manes
thin ribbons that never tear
sunrise, sunset
simple duties they never lose.

III.

Stars are the only markers where you travel
setting your course for the next month
all this hard work of staying alive.

Planets whisper in their orbits
tell you the secret of flying through air
defying the gravity created to keep
every part of you on the ground
closer to the lower depths
the fire and water.

Old woman, iron woman
nothing can hold you
your chants will be heard in heaven
bitter rantings of the mouth
as it soars near the edges of clouds.

The Flight

Evil no evil
carry me devil
when the moon is new
and darkness ancient
I fly in my mortar
and steer with my pestle
to Wysah Mountain
home of my grandfather
to the swift, white river
where my sister lives
to deep ravines
where herbs and roots grow
to an empty soul
at the edge of madness
to a proud heart
cold and waiting
to a silent child
lost in the woods
to an adultress
brushing her hair
to the farmer
broken and desolate
to his wife
alone in bed

Evil no evil
carry me devil
I fly with the dark clouds
sweeping away my tracks
with an old birch broom
so you cannot see
where I have been
only the stars know
as my wild hair
whips them into silence.

The Abandoned Children

I am their adopted mother
can tell when they begin life
the slow journey no one touches
footprints deep in the woods
they come to me begging
to sit by the fire

I see them with red eyes
my fingers pierce their small places

When they finally enter my hut
their shadows vanish
their bodies melt into mine
their ghosts become the leaves
covering my feet.

The Peasant Woman Tells How Baba Yaga
Took Her Grandmother

I can hear you laughing in your house
the foundations shaking and you
wrapped in animal skins wanting her
closer, your breath in her mouth
closer.

Grandmother opened the door, let you in
she fed you beet soup and dark bread
you waited for the sign to appear
the beautiful black flower growing
out of her own mouth.

I remember you gave her
new shoes for the funeral
and took a strand of hair
to sew her lips tight
stitching it back
and forth until
her silence was complete.

The Chant of the Three Sisters

We live in our magic
in the center of the earth
the power of our hands
not as great as hers
elder sister
the old one
but we know all her secrets
waters of life
waters of death
what lives in her hair
where she keeps her soul
we know all her secrets
the circle she weaves
the fire she steals
what walks in her dreams
who is her lover
how long is her life
we know all her secrets
let them grow
let them live
these secrets, her secrets

Baba Yaga Tells the Story of the Hanged Man

He married the rope-maker's daughter
and she tried to teach him to fly
from the very top of an old oak
placing a noose around his neck
to support his head, while his arms
and legs grabbed the air. Everyone
knows how the tale ends, how his wife
yelled at him to speak—she only saw
the thick tongue slowly turning black.

This is my favorite story. I tell it often
to the moon, to the trees, to my victims
even the ravens listen closely to every word
as if trying to imagine this man's soft eyes
how his shoulder feels hard under their claws.

The Reader Speaks to Baba Yaga

I used to dream about you
old woman without a face
shadow moving closer
sounds of thin birds
leave your throat
audible through sleep
through hands pressed over ears.

Those almost silent dreams
where you create children
instead of destroying them
where you shape hearts
paint the veins magenta
or just red without the blue
then mold enough flesh
to fit the skin you stretch
over bones, over teeth.

I see the bodies, bleached shells
they wait to be filled
their names marked.

You gather these children
from a distance you call
speak the names
mine, the first.

The Night Song

She is Queen of Night, reigning over
mountains, valleys, river-beds
those holes in your hand that stare out as you sleep
the small grin hiding inside your closet
she is there, she is there
waiting to freeze you in a glance
her iron tits hanging
cold flesh on bones
gaunt arms extended in welcome
you have seen her
the first vision to greet you out of the womb
you have heard her
the high pitch of the storm as it rocks the house
her gray teeth singing

I am Mother
I am Mother

Lullaby

The witch will not eat you
nor silver wolves carry you off
and the evil step-mother will be locked away
in her beauty, her mirrors, and her song.

Curled into soft bones that will last forever
stay safe and deep inside me
close your eyes in my darkness
the light will come soon enough.

Under the Rim of the World

Initiation

There are birds that fly
under the rim of the world
giving it a push;
only a woman in childbirth
can hear their wings.

Sestina: Grandma

I am four years old and the air is sweat,
the basement walls dripping. I hold her hand
and go down the steps, down, my eyes
wide in my head. I see the edge of the knife
as it gleams, as she caresses and strokes
my hair. "Only a woman

can do this," she says to the woman
in me. I can feel myself sweat
the victim looks at me. Feathers I stroke
smooth in the dark, soft in a small hand
that doesn't forget. But Grandma knows the knife
will jump, has seen this day with eyes

has felt it for years before my eyes
left the body of her son's woman.
This day I am old enough to see the knife
dance on the throat, a duck's sweat
the perfect soup that hands
pray over. "You must stroke

its neck gently, gently as if each stroke
was a kiss." Grandma looks calm, eyes
far away in Europe, remembering a hand
on her neck, her blouse. Only a woman
can do this, can cut so clean that sweat
becomes air, a lover. The knife

she holds will talk in my dreams. "Knife,
dance with me, dance." She strokes
the blade again, again until sweat
dulls it. I stare and all the babies' eyes
deep within me, stare. Every woman
can draw blood slow, can fill her hands.

"Grandma, I love you, I love your hands,"
the duck's throat pumps the words. Knife
inherits the blood, all the sad women
who drown in it. Their wild strokes
embrace the walls, their eyes
crazy songs wide with sweat.

Only a woman can do this, can stroke
so gentle. Her hands for thirty years knife
her eyes almost silent. They listen. Sweat.

Forgiving the Dead

After you've been dead
for over twenty years,
I finally dream of you.
Bone-white, sunk in your bed
the lung cancer already digging
its tight-fisted cave
into your chest.

Your thin arms rise
to embrace me and
your one good eye
fakes a wink. You grin
with brown teeth,
the smell of Canadian Club
and Chesterfields. Like always.
And the broken English,
like always, is scolding me:
"Hurry up and die
so I have you here
for talking." You're alone
in starched whiteness–
your skin, the bed, the room.
In heaven, nothing has changed.

And for an instant, I
almost forgive you
everything. How you ignored
my father and his words
so completely that
now language eludes him.
How you accused your only daughter
of stealing her voice
from gypsies, from peddlars
of rags because you
couldn't understand
what she said. How you
screamed at your wife
with such shrill faithfulness
that for years after your death
she grew to hate silence.

In another part of this dream
you are eighteen
and not yet foreign. America is not
even brooding in the background
with its steel mills,
gray houses, dead-end streets.
You stand in the long grasses
by the river outside Krakow
and start undressing a woman
for the first time. There
is no sound in heaven
but the deep expanse
of your breathing
trying to fill the empty sky.

Back in Montana

My father never knew me back in Montana.
I recognized him good, out of one eye
knowing the photograph probably lied.
His body young, careless, part of the land.
He thought hitching into town from the mountain
the big event of the winter. And the ice
agreed. It was the Depression. Only cold air
was in abundance, filling up every man.

Now my father's Montana days are done.
He can still see Butte when it was three lights
but he cannot remember being young.
And he yells and he yells, "Too much night
is bad for your skin. Where are the trees, the sun?"
The photograph doesn't answer, just holds the sky.

The Fear of Vacuum Cleaners

for my son

Ah, little one of the deep fish-eye,
little dreamer of the night and the day

and the night. You stare at this new
world of air, earth, and light,

wonder at the simplest things.
How a green tendril can sprout

from black ground. The deafening
sound a vacuum cleaner makes.

A sound you cannot bear
to hear: terror of the deep wind

sucking you up into a dark
place that holds no memory.

Legend says the still unborn
can see with closed eyes, possess

a look of surprise as they
peer from thin sacs covering

their shrunken bodies like shrouds
or wedding veils. Ah, little one,

when the vacuum cleaner looms
from its black closet-home

and you cannot blink your eyes,
do you remember the legend?

Staring at the Brick Wall

In the basement of a contemporary
art museum, there's a plain
brick wall that some artist
took over. He drilled holes,
bore into the brick and mortar.
In the empty spaces he created,
he placed miniature dwellings,
tiny adobe villages–
a Mesa Verde that only
dolls could inhabit.
If I stare at this wall
for a long time, I can see
a tiny face flash past
a tiny window. I can imagine
anything.

I sit here and imagine
my father who's never
been in a museum–
let alone Mesa Verde. If he
saw this, he'd probably think
real people lived in this wall,
got married, raised children,
lost their jobs, died.

I sit here and imagine
your middle son who
can do nothing but
bang his head against
a brick wall of his own
careful making because
that's the only way
he can love himself.

And I imagine your trip
to the Anasazi villages.
The shock of seeing Cliff Palace
materialize out of nowhere,
your countless pictures
of the reddish-brown walls. And
that one of your husband
trying to climb out
of the kiva but not
quite making it. A metaphor,
you joked, for mid-life
crisis, male menopause.
A confusion as real
as witnessing purple verbena
blossom from sandstone.

I sit here and imagine
all the men in our lives
who balance their lives
like the ancient cliff-
dwellers. Back and forth
they travel to those remote
alcoves under the surface
where even the heart
is afraid. They call to us,
tell us not to worry, describe
their lives like seasoned explorers.
Unchanging as the desert sky.
Steady as the growth of juniper.
Elaborate as the perfect wall
constructed by primitive men
who could not have known better.

To the Younger Sister in Love

I can't tell you anything
you don't already know:
how a man sweats
when you're under him
and the smell that sticks
to your skin afterward;
how the bitterness that broods
when he's not with you
roots itself in the heart,
grows out of your hands,
then lunges for the throat.

Yet those nights in bed,
your legs joined to his hip,
you can only think of the hair
on your arms or how peculiar
his ass looks or what shoes
you'll wear tomorrow at noon.

And when you dream, you grow
cat's fur—claw the carpet,
leave traces of your teeth
on my white arm that remembers
holding a girl who climbed trees,
not men.

I feel my breath being sucked away
when I realize men in the street
know you better; their eyes
settle on some part of your body,
ignore my rouge, mascara, the simple
gesture you have begun to master.

Heat Lightning

for Theresa Becker

The jagged lines of bluish gray were nothing
but God taking pictures at night.
Just his flashbulbs going off,
mother said. In other words–
harmless, temporary–like everything
that could ever fade from your life.

No thunder came with this lightning.
It was always silent and horizontal,
never touching the ground, only
mutely racing across the sky.
A futile attempt to reach
a destination that wasn't there,
like a hapless runner racing
toward the gate of heaven.

And mother would whisper:
Things that can't touch you,
can't hurt you. Such a whole-
some lie; I wanted to believe
it and almost did. Letting
the words lull me into a dream
where sparrows had no wings,
fathers had no arms, the petals
of dahlias closed like the tight
shutters, and the black sky seemed
torn into a million shreds.
Each shred tiny and lost,
a discarded negative, unable
to imagine something whole.

In the morning when I awoke,
it was as if God had vanished
along with his camera. No trace
of that quiet lightning going
nowhere. Just the unbroken
blue of the sky. And the round
sun looking relieved, a bit tired,
like the face in an old photograph:
an aunt long-dead whose name
no one remembers. Whose face
looks familiar but untouchable.

A Horse Under A Sky

You first paint the amber-red
mare. The color of dark blood.
You then invent a yellow sky and
the short bursts of her breath
reaching to the edge of the paper
which has no line of horizon.

The horse seems to fly
in this rectangular universe—
hooves extended, mere hint of brown
wings. Steam rises from her back
and she waits. Hopes for green
hay, apples, the movement of your
small hand on the page.

Son, this is a picture
of the world before you were born.
One flying horse suspended
under one yellow sky. No visible
line of land to touch down on.
No idea of direction, destination,
of coming from, or going to.
Only solid space, blank
and shining. Totally yours.

The Widow's Occupation

Dead plants inhabit my house
take up space, collect dust.

Their yellowed stems prove
a faithfulness. These wandering jews

can never leave; maidenhair
ferns show more delicacy dead than alive.

(How the brown fronds weep
when I touch them). The azaleas

haven't bloomed in years. I like them
better this way–like a clothesline

in the attic, its dried white cracking
and I never have to worry about rain.

Dead things last forever: pressed
baby's breath lingers; my rosary

vine dies in my hands; and one
deliberate death looks like another.

Maybe I should take up gardening,
kill the thing at its roots.

Aunt from West Virginia

For sixteen years she thought the sky was lost
in orange, not in blue. The steel mills owned
her life completely, blindly, even down
to colors. How the laundry smouldered rust
on lines, on shelves, on faceless men she pursed
her lips for. Empty days when light and sun
got clogged in valleys, turned out bad and wrong.
Like sisters, pregnant, skins becoming coarse.

The last years now belong to husband: some-
one boring, clean, from Midwest plains. Her hair
just slightly gray, she fills her house with prisms.
So many colors she can hold in her
pale hand. Unlike the stillborn infants, mum
and blue. Unlike the air: uncolored, clear.

The Change

At fifty, she's the quick-change
artist resembling anything but herself.
Even her shadow becomes nothing more
than a thin cape stitched in place by air.
Her body assumes the posture
of a stranger while the children
grow away, the husband simply
leaves and she's stranded holding
a picture of her once ripe cervix.
A tiny mouth with slick lips,
bubbles along its edge. Probably
cancer, but she keeps the picture,
frames it on her bedroom wall,
anoints it with moist breath.
Her body now stops flowing red,
rarely flows white unlike those two
lucky princesses named after the two
rosebushes growing in the backyard.

Her body now creates its own
fairy tale. She groups holy cards
in families of eight. She saves
the dust that settles on the blue
Virgin's head. She knows her soul
inhabits the eyes of mute dogs.
She wears red lipstick. Redder.
Reddest. Until her wild, loud
face becomes slowly dormant:
the perfect smooth and quiet of mask.

Men as Fathers

If the stars are nothing but examples
of how hard it is to kill the past,
and the unfinished book on the shelf
becomes another stone in your true arsenal
of guilt; if every sound that escapes
your lips is a deep moan, a sigh,
a fall from grace that every woman
in your life warned you about;
if your heart has fled to the border
where an uneasy truce covers barbed wire
with raw silk, where the neon in bars
looks alive and trapped; in other words,
if you desire your life, then its design
will appear overhead in the night sky,
a constellation of white forming
the thin blade before it breaks the ice,
or the face of your daughter: quiet, asleep.

My Son Expounds on His Theory of Creation

In the beginning,
before the birth of God, there was nothing. No word,
no sound, not even silence. Just a vastness as deep
and empty as the desert at night.

The first man
and the first woman came out of this vastness, rising
from the dirt like some wild, deliberate dust storm:
bone, muscle, an arm, a leg, teeth, hair.
They began their lives like ageless clocks,
with no sense of the past. They began their lives
together, reflecting nothing but the present–
the imagination of the other.

And with this
imagination, they created all manner of living things.
Cactus and Queen Anne's lace. Tree frog and toadstool.
Chartreuse moray and gray trout. Ruby-throated humming-
bird and masked shrew. Triceratops and cave man. All
manner of living things they created.

And then they
created death (so life could continue) by giving birth
to a pale girl who could neither hear nor speak but only
stare as she collected the dying souls like small, rare
postage stamps from a foreign country.

The first man
and the first woman then rested, because they thought
by creating life and death, the universe was complete.
But something was missing–something invisible yet
tangible. The man and the woman could not imagine angels.
Pure spirit eluded them.

So they decided to take all
the dead animals that anyone ever loved and make them
angels. The old collie that died in Mrs. Blazek's arms—
a seraphim. The green parakeet that sang for Mr. Kivela—
an archangel. The small turtle that lived in a box
in the corner of Joey's room—a cherubim.

                              Listen well, Mother.
Because when I leave you to create my own life in my own world,
and your heart breaks because I am no longer yours,
and your body aches for the child who has left it,
and your mind can do nothing but stay in the same empty room—
do not worry.

              My guardian angel will be with me always,
as real as he was when he walked among us: Sam, our Siamese
cat, protecting my every move. His blue eyes will be calm
and omniscient like that one day you held him in your lap
and he felt the baby kick inside of you. The complete
and utter improbability. The shock of new life.

Prose Poems: A History of the Body

Blood

for Pete

Dark and blind, the blood owns nothing but memory, the cold
knowledge of its origins. And the man who wants to drain that
memory from his body, who refuses to listen to its voice, will
inevitably sink in its calm but treacherous currents. He will
never understand how the blood's memory enters him and
changes his soul from the deep blue of the umbilicus to the
flashing scarlet of his own peculiar life. It is the life that is
reflected in the blood–the tangible river that perpetuates the
history as well as the legend of a family. The father with the
nicotine stains between his fingers who took a quick death
before sixty. The mother with the tendency toward migraines
who bathes in holy water. The uncle from Colorado found
frozen to death searching for his lost cattle. The aunt who
drank herself into oblivion. And the blood remembers every
detail of these lives, every nuance of these deaths, as it
surrounds each cell of the man trying to forget. What he wants
is solid night. No dreams. Soon he will rouse from his fitful
sleep, remember the wordless lullaby that filled so many
nights with lilac, soft muslin. Soon he will rise and go to
awaken his daughters as they lie dreaming of men who will
enter them.

Skin Nodule

This history is not a real history but merely a semblance of one. The skin nodule is notorious for its many disguises— harmless beauty mark, threatening melanoma. It tries to make a living by altering the skin's outline, by attempting to push epidermal cells out of the body and into the air. Nodules come in many shapes and colors but can be found only on certain people: those whose skin has become bored or those who sweat too much and grow nodules to conceal their pores. Pregnant women and their fathers are the most frequently afflicted. The women, because their skin doesn't belong to them anymore and they desperately create nodules to keep themselves preoccupied. The fathers, becauses they have no chance of becoming anything else and the sight of their impregnated daughters makes them nervous, embarrassed, even jealous.

Navel

Every mother knows that her child's navel is actually a scar–a scar from her own body that formed when the baby tore away. This tearing leaves a hole in the mother, generally found in the gut, but more recently it has been discovered in the heart, close to dead center, or even in the second toe of the left foot. Some mothers try to cover up this hole with cosmetics, tight sweaters, and leather boots. While others, realizing the importance of sacrifice, gradually become the hole inside of them–throwing bits and pieces of themselves into it until nothing is left. Nothing except the shadow of the original scar as it sinks deeper and deeper into the bodies of their children.

Toenails

A quiet, shy character (a male poet) in an American short story insists that toenails grow wild and uncontrollable in East Europe. There, they do not need conscious thought to thrive and flourish. They do it in spite of themselves, without thinking. He feels this part of the world is the only place where history really does matter and, in effect, allows the toenail to be nothing more, nothing less than a toenail. In Poland, Czechoslovakia, Hungary, and Romania, old women sift through oppression in tight shoes, binding stockings and never bother to cut their toenails; they know it is the one part of themselves that is forever replenishing. A prime example—my grandmother from Krakow. Wild and uncontrollable at 86, she cursed her Cleveland-born sons and decided to live in the attic. Finally, she ran away from home in late January with no shoes, her bare feet clicking on the ice. The sound of hard, blue toenails long and curved over the edge of the toes like naturally fitted tap shoes. And the last image she left me was of her dancing out a little secret code spelling VISTULA, ZAKOPANE, TATRA, JASNA GORA. Take off your shoes and learn it, she said.

Hand

for Frank Niemiec

History of the ditch digger, stone mason, countless men in factories, on the line. History of abundance, of miracles because it is by our hands that we become who we are. "Marry a man for his hands," my father said. Probably remembering his own father and the mangled right hand that was torn in half by the machine at the woolen mill. But what did the old man know about machines? He was a foreigner who couldn't speak the language, a peasant farmer born in Poland when it wasn't even called Poland. His hands knew only two things: black earth and how to coax the miracle of green from it. Each spring he would perform the miracle in his small American garden. His left hand did the mundane chore of clearing the winter's debris, breaking the ground with hoe and shovel and pickaxe. His right hand–that terrible, wondrous hand– performed the ultimate magic: placed each seed in its proper spot, made sure it grew into a cabbage or pepper or summer squash. I remember how carefully he would wash that hand after the day's work. Pat it dry. Place it almost casually on my shoulder. Luminous, enchanted.

Lungs

When the first living creature left the sea forever and took its first breath, the lungs became arrogant. They wanted to claim total responsibility for the evolution that abandoned the gills and produced the nose. This arrogance belied their humble beginnings in small, damp rooms and the endless string of boring jobs. However, when the lungs tasted air, they began to despise their past. And later, when they grew to perfection in man, they began to fear it. Somehow the lungs knew they could never go back–that any nostalgia would destroy them. It is this nostalgia that causes a death by drowning. The corpse, purple and bloated, transcends its human perimeters. The face assumes an expansive look that can only be attributed to pure wisdom. And the lungs, purged of their arrogance, content themselves with growing seaweed and recalling how tight the tendrils grasp.

Ears

A mere accident of birth to have ears like dried sea shells–
spiralled whorls leading to dimly lit caves that soon forget the
ocean's roar. But to possess the highly deliberate ears of Joan
of Arc. To be able to hear distinct voices in the rustling of
leaves, in the ringing of church bells. Voices belonging to
Catherine of Alexandria, Margaret of Antioch, Michael of
Heaven. To distinguish the exotic foreign languages–especially
that celestial tongue that hasn't been invented yet. The words
breathe in the ear, telling you to forget your life, the possibility
of a husband, the red, patched dress. You believed, and in
exchange received men's clothing, short hair, male companions
as soldiers not lovers, a dullard posing as king. Not to mention
the incomprehensible thunder from the Church asking: "What
language did your voice speak?" And your quiet reply: "A better
one than yours." That a woman could hear so much and know
exactly what is meant proved to be your fatal flaw–hearing
better than the men around you. So they tried to dismiss you
as a frivolous army mascot. And when that didn't work, the
trumped-up charge, phony trial, forced conviction. You
wouldn't let your hair grow long or put on a dress or cover
your ears to the voices predicting the rush of wind, roar of
flames. Only the paper dunce cap of the convicted witch–
marked Heretic, Relapsed, Apostate, Idolatress–that you were
forced to wear at the burning was mute.

Teeth

Even before birth, teeth know their destiny. For the most part, it's predictable: grow up, get a job, leave town, come back, develop a tendency for the needle and drill, and eventually, leave town for good. Only a few teeth are ever remembered. For instance, Josephine, Napoleon's first wife, had terrible teeth. The empress of France, cursed with rotten teeth in a tiny mouth, never laughed. Napoleon tried to overlook this and would say, *"Mais Cherie, tu as une personalite tres atachant."** He bought her a country house outside Paris and planted 250 kinds of roses in her back yard for her to sniff at whim. No good. Her teeth still hurt. That's why Napoleon was frequently away from home and in such far-flung places as Cairo, Austerlitz, Marengo, Somosierra. Josephine's teeth made him quite adept in killing men and stealing land. He was a success. But 13 years of closed-mouth kissing prompted him to divorce Jospehine for an Austrian girl who was a bit scatter-brained but had gorgeous teeth. These teeth made Napoleon so happy that he lost all compulsion to work–*i.e.* he began to lose battles and soon got himself exiled. Josephine continued to live in the Parisian suburbs, refusing to smile, pruning her roses in fine, white gloves, hoping the thorns would bite deep enough.

*translation: But Dear, you have such a winning personality.

Hair

for Kathleen

I am the part of you that you never need. This insignificance forces every strand to be preposterous, outrageous. Like three jet-black pubic hairs casually perched on the margarine dish in the refrigerator. Primary evidence of how easy it is to leave a part of yourself behind. And, in a blink of an eyelash, you are everywhere: the kitchen drain, another woman's shoulders, the spinach salad, a vacant house 200 miles away. Look closely. I am always and never with you. As obstinate and abstract as the white hair locked into the ice cube floating in the bourbon glass. Your bourbon, your ice cube. Whose hair? If you persist in knowing the mysteries of the obvious—what you always lay claim to but never possess—I will if pulled tight enough, divulge the answer. But first, you must wait fifty years until I change color or disappear. Now. Now, you can begin to collect the particulars of your life.

Fingers

How they were born with an obsession for counting. The number of walls in a room, the number of clouds in the sky. But fingers became tired of dealing with the obvious and started to concentrate on subtle things. Bottles of perfume, pairs of shoes, gray hairs. Their compulsion grew geometrically: "Why should we be compulsive about just one thing when we can be compulsive about ten," they said. Even the purest of abstractions fell prey to their greasy touch: *e.g.* obtuse angles, null sets, the diameters of the moon during the vernal equinox. But for sheer obsession, no fingers can match the poet's fingers. They grow skinnier each year from their counting. They lose gold rings and forget they ever wore them. Theirs is the loneliest profession; none of them knows the others exist.

Tongue

Like flowers that first grew in the ground when pterodactyls became extinct, our tongues began as fragile buds–fragrant, harmless. They rooted only in select places, changed colors from vermillion to indigo in autumn, died quietly in winter. After millenia of cultivation, we finally learned how to loosen the tongue from the earth; we transplanted the bud to the dank caverns of the mouths and forced it to embrace and tame the air escaping our bodies. We began to speak. Vowels and consonants, diphthongs and syllables, words. Language flourished, became polished and refined, took over all transactions from the genteel to the coarse. No longer a possession of the few, the tongue became commonplace: in other words, ordinary; in other words, contemptible. Now tongues grow everywhere, shaking their thick stems. Especially in small towns where they turn into the very gossip they love so well. Curling like vines around the ex-husband, drunk and naked, who shouts obscenities at midnight. Curling around the ex-wife, restless and awake, who paces the floor around and around the hushed rooms.

Breasts

The mountains that divide men from women. Geography
rather than history: plateau, summits, the gentle slopes
leading to lush valleys. Only women are blessed with such
richness, and men, since time immemorial, have wanted to
take possession. Not because of lust or wantonness, but
because their bodies never owned anything as constant, as
predictable. Thus, the battle between the sexes began
primarily over territory; land was power, words were cheap,
and no one trusted anyone. The male/female differential grew
more and more apparent. It seemed no force on earth could
bridge the gap. Then suddenly, one clear morning that was
filled with nothing but devastating blue, the strange tension
erupted. Islands sank into the ocean while new subcontinents
arose from the sea's depths like Botticelli's Venus: landmasses
started to shift; continental shelves collided; earthquakes split
like dress seams. Men and women began to fall in love.

Penis

This history is as changeable as the styles of the architect, the real molder of men who built Stonehenge, the massive columns of the Acropolis, the mismatched but somehow correct twin spires of Chartres Cathedral. It is as unpredictable as the little known phallus of the Tower of Babel leading to nowhere. From these, the penis has attained a design that at times is so irrational that it defies analysis, even with the aid of illustrated sex manuals. Better to stick with the architect's blueprints, diagrams of perspective, the solid hard hat at the job site. Forget soft feminine form. All buildings are analogous to only one kind of body: the upright male enclosed in wood/fitted sod/mud/brick/concrete/glass/steel. The accommodating sheath that expands and contracts depending on the life blood within. To enter this sheath is to enter a secret and primordial place. Where the architect's tools lie uninvented. Where lost, untouched bodies languish in the condemned tenement house.

Heart

for Faye Kicknosway

Living the vicious lie that the heart is the center of love, we are all guilty of promoting the mirage: this false history of transformation that turns men into wild swine, women into winged beasts with hoarse voices, love into the mere idea of love. No totems can dispel the lie. Not Garbo with men imprisoned in her nonchalant body like speared fish. Not Grable with the straight black seams running down her legs. Not even Venus looking academic and time-conscious with a torn heart where her perfect breast should be. And who is that calm, anonymous lady wearing an impersonal heart instead of a face? Is she the one sure sign of the final moment when the heart beats the wildest? In death. Not love. Friend, let us be truthful about our lives; we will never eat rose hips arranged in a valentine. Just barely hear the monotonous echoes of our blood moving from the divided chambers to our fingers, tired lips.

Back

The huge dream of ourselves that will never be realized. Like a map whose topography is best known to strangers because we cannot see the immense reaches and boundless extremes of what is always behind us. This bewildering place without shadows, constant repetition of white on glaring white. The back as Antarctica of the body: ice sheets and collapsing glacial tongues between the shoulder blades. Here, we can experience the most violent winds on the planet and never turn around. The exotic names we give the unknown regions of our world and ourselves are testaments to our pristine ambivalence. Cape Wild. Longitudinal ligament. Dry Valleys. Slipped discs. Deception Island. The ever-present vertebrae that are no more than melting ice cliffs. Our backs might as well be at the bottom of the world. Nothing on the other side but raw beauty, silence.

Armpit

Now we enter the deep pit of our desires, the root of all lust. Its smell provided our ancestors' first lesson in mating and thus our first history. The salt taste of the ocean, our birthplace; the salt taste of sweat on flesh. But civilization has defined the armpit as an embarrassment, has tried to masquerade it as an object of boredom–creased, closed, hidden. The armpit as luke-warm sex after 17 years of marriage. The armpit shaved and perfumed into impotence. Women who hold their lovers between their legs–who appear like familiar litanies on street corners, black-haired whores in Barcelona– know the true importance of the uncensored armpit. The delicate, vulnerable flesh underneath the wild shock of hair, hair that shows the true color of the body. And it is here, in the deepness of the armpit, that we learn the concave absence of love. The hollow place blind passion attempts to fill again and again.

Sweat

Look for it in the Midwest where sweat was really invented and patented. You'll find it alive, thriving in Mitch Ryder, the one person who can sweat more than anyone. Even without the back-up of the Detroit Wheels. Even when he lip-syncs. Like a dinosaur in heat Mitch lumbers on the stage. Sings the same song, the only song he will ever be remembered for. Sweat of the fossil glides down his neck. Back in 1966, we were sweating, too. If not on the dance floor with Mitch's grunts blaring from the speakers, then in the back seat of some guy's Ford. Devil with the blue dress on . . . or off. But no boy furtively holding me in a slow dance embrace or in a parked car where the air became the moisture escaping our bodies–no boy ever sweated like Mitch sweated. And for all I know, Ryder was more real, more alive, more wet than any guy who unbuttoned my blouse or parted my legs. The car radio playing that one song. The same, calculated Ryder-sweat: steaming into translucent drops that formed on the windows of the gold '63 Thunderbird; steaming into the sweat of whoever it was that tried to make me that night.

Legs

Forget the platonic preoccupation with imagery of bone,
metaphor of heart. In the hard world of the real world, every
living poet favors the legs over any other part of the body. This
love affair begins at the crease of knee, climaxes in mid-calf,
and doesn't end until it reaches the bony island of the ankle.
Men's legs, women's legs arouse the same sensual journey. Like
the Queen of Sheba's celebrated visit to Solomon: and behold,
he fell in love with her legs (being the true poet that he was).
No matter that they were covered with coarse Arabian hair.
No matter that she came to him merely to obtain a secret
depilatory recipe and certainly not to fall in love. Regardless of
what that awful 1959 movie would have us believe. But who
would believe Yul Brynner as Solomon wearing a greasy
Hollywood hairpiece? And who would believe Gina
Lollobrigida as Sheba with shaved legs and a ruby in her
navel, dancing like a college freshman? Only middle-aged poets
with eyes glued to the screen. Bodies motionless, legs crossed.

Eye

Consider the eye as a tiny balloon growing out of the front of your brain. Or your iris as the colored ring of brown-green stone surrounding the pupil, that ultimate and quiet black hole. Consider the light that the blackness swallows and never returns. But these visions of the public eye–the eye that belongs to everyone, even the lowliest sewer rat stuck underneath some gray city–do nothing but bore you. You would rather consider the very private eye. A loner just this side of the law hired by a sleek, rich woman to find a pair of diamond earrings lost in some posh casino. And before long, a corpse is dumped into the back seat of your hero's black DeSoto. Is it Louie, the brooding casino owner, or Mr. X, the rich woman's long-forgotten husband? Or did she ever have a husband? And why is she offering the unhandsome detective cases of bourbon, cartons of Chesterfields, endless nights alone with her cologne-cool body? You slowly realize, long before the hero does, that all of it is a hoax. The earrings, the corpse, the casino, the broad. Even the hero. The only true image you can believe is the oily, black street down which the DeSoto now dissolves. Into night. Into nothing. Your eyes will never become accustomed to the light.

Cold Sore

It comes out of nowhere, but usually nowhere is either your lower lip or your right nostril or–God forbid–your genitals. In the first two instances the herpes is designated as simplex but the last location always makes the cold sore complicated. Overnight it changes its name to cunt sore or cock sore and begins to lead a glamorous, hectic life. Graduates from Vassar write books about it, countless reporters seek interviews, Phil Donahue persuades it to appear on his T.V. show. Next week it will invest in a disco franchise and become fashionable. Meanwhile, the cold sore on your lip stays home and makes meat loaf for dinner. It thinks: tomorrow is a good day to clean the basement. It will never vacation in the Bahamas during winter.

Bowels

for Dick Jansma

All the angels and saints clapped in heaven when the bowels
got religion. From mindless caves of intestinal tract they
blossomed into catacombs, the holiest part of the body, the
place to bury the sainted dead: St. Sam, lover of Irish women;
St. Buck, the insomniac; St. Calvin of the bulging wallet; St.
Bruce, the renegade pope; St. Marilyn of Minnesota; St. Carol
of the rare cookbooks; St. Dee, the desirable. This litany goes
on and on. Feeds on itself until it is exhausted, until the
bowels cannot hold any more relics. And finally, puffed-up with
sainthood, they become irritable and petty, sour and mean. All
that the bowels really wanted was the simple life: a nice
house, a new suit, a clean precise end.

Feet

Vanity begins here, at the bottom. Whether left or right, feet are equally proud, evasive, never claiming to belong to the body they are attached to. They may try to look interested in the welfare of the whole, but are so removed from the center of things–the hub of activity–that even the body doesn't know when they are missing. Like small musical instruments it tends to misplace. Remember that scene in "Thunderball" where Sean Connery kisses the foot of an almost nude woman on the beach? Claudia Something. The name is not important, her body is not important, but that foot is. Already it forgets her, becomes a light harmonica in Sean's hands. Cold, damp metal on his lips–the taste of the ocean's salt. The sun sets–the music swells. And her footprints in the sand dissolve, sink back into what they are not. No trace of them or their vanity, except in some treadworn corner of Hollywood where they are ceremoniously imprisoned in the cement.

Bones

for Rebecca

X-rays uncover the real you that hides in darkness, the faint
shadow of your body as you sleep. When the bones dream, they
leave no forwarding address but choose to reincarnate as
flights of birds near the coast. Your hip evolves into a wing,
your knee, a beak, your foot, a pale eye. The marrow
relinquishes its grayness to sprout feathers of every color
imaginable–green, orange, violet, yellow. Even the space
between your joints is lost as it unfolds into the smooth
motion of flight itself. But in the waking world, your bones
remain submerged in your body; they can do nothing but stay
in place. Their one hope is that their condition is not
permanent, that one day they will abandon their home and
never return. Only then will you remember the birds. How
wildly they beat their wings. Their song so pure and intense
you almost wish you had never heard it.

Body

for my daughter

Body within my body, I shape you out of almost nothing, give
you a tight envelope to surround your soul. I deem you female–
eyes cobalt blue, fingers long and translucent–without even
realizing it. And after the quantum leap from single cell to
complex organism, much of your body's life is beyond my
conscious thought: your waking, your sleeping, the small
objects of your complete desire. Complete as the perfect wings
of the jay above your head or the pale stars that mark your
birth with nothing but pure light. Daughter, I cannot give you
anything so complete or perfect or pure. But I can give you
something better. Your body, which is your life. And the fierce
love of it that no one can take away. And these words that will
remind you of that love. And your father's broad hand that
opened the door to it. And the blankness of the rest of this page
for your own words, your own history.

About the Author

Linda Nemec Foster received her M.F.A. in creative writing from Goddard College (Vermont) and currently lives in Grand Rapids. Her poems have been widely published in such journals as *The Georgia Review, Indiana Review, Nimrod, Pennsylvania Review, University of Windsor Review, Mid-American Review,* and *Quarterly West.* Her translations (with Beata Kane) of the Polish poet, Ewa Parma, have appeared in *Artful Dodge* and *International Poetry Review.* Foster's work has also been anthologized in *Contemporary Michigan Poetry* (Wayne State University Press), *Passages North Anthology* (Milkweed Editions), *Women of the 14th Moon* (Crossing Press), and *Catholic Girls* (Penguin/Plume). Her poetry has appeared in translation in one of Poland's leading literary journals, *Literatura.* Foster has received two Creative Artist Grants for her poetry from the Michigan Council for the Arts, a grant from The Arts Foundation of Michigan, and fifteen Pushcart Prize nominations. She is the author of three chapbooks: *A History of the Body* (Coffee House Press), *A Modern Fairy Tale: The Baba Yaga Poems* (Ridgeway Press), and *Trying to Balance the Heart* (Sun Dog Press). *Living in the Fire Nest* is her first full-length collection of poems and was a finalist for the Bluestem Poetry Award. Currently she helps coordinate the literature program for the Urban Institute for Contemporary Arts in Grand Rapids, Michigan.

Judy Hillman
Book Design

Dana Freeman
Front Cover Art

Robert Turney
Back Cover Photo

Joyce Clay
Manuscript Typist

Amy Van Hove
Typesetter

Switzerland Narrow + Century Schoolbook
Typeface

Seaman Mohawk Options 80lb cover
Simpson Coronado 80lb text
Simpson Quest 80lb cover sheets
Paper

1996

DATE DUE